REBUILD YOUR TEMPLE
GOD'S WAY®

FAITH AND HEALTH DEVOTIONAL

A 30-DAY JOURNEY TO HOLISTIC HEALTH AND WHOLENESS

STEPHANIE L. FRANKLIN-SUBER

Dedication

To my faithful and steadfast husband, **Berchard V. Suber**, and to my son, **Michael Franklin Suber**—thank you for your resolute and unswerving love, prayers, and devotion throughout my nearly twenty-year journey to reclaim and maintain a life of health and wholeness.

Through cancer, chronic illness, and cardiac arrest, you walked beside me with perseverance, resilience, and courage. You are my beacons of hope and inspiration—daily reminders that love endures all things and that the mercy, compassion, and grace of our triune God truly sustain.

To **Reverend Anna Grant-Borden** and the members of **Mount Airy Presbyterian Church**, past, present, and future—may you be blessed for your faithful prayers, support, and partnership in ministry.

To every woman on the journey to health and wholeness—may this *Rebuild Your Temple, God's Way® Faith and Health Devotional* and the companion *Faith and Health Devotional Bible Study Workbook* become a sacred space of reverence, reflection, and revelation as you walk on this 30-day journey with the God who makes all things new.

May you discover the beauty of *Rebuilding Your Temple, God's Way®*.

With utmost gratitude to my **Heavenly Father**, my Creator, to my **Lord and Savior**, **Jesus Christ**, and to the **Holy Spirit**, whose power restores, renews and aligns us—body, soul, and spirit.

May You be glorified.

Blessed by the support of Cathy Morenzie, Preston Squire, and Jennifer Eastmond, and by the gifted work of Alec Gerhart and Rachel Aponte.

Foreword

Do you not know that your body is a temple of the Holy Spirit who is within you, whom you have from God, and that you are not your own? You were bought with a price [you were actually purchased with the precious blood of Jesus and made His own]. So then, honor and glorify God with your body.
(1 Corinthians 6:19–20 AMP)

Our bodies are sacred edifices, masterfully created by God for His glory and for worship. In Psalm 19:1, King David declares, *"The heavens declare the glory of God; the skies proclaim the work of his hands."* Just as the heavens reflect the majesty of God, so do we — His beloved creation. We are the workmanship of His hands, *"fearfully and wonderfully made."*

Yet as we journey through life, the demands placed on our bodies — some self-imposed and others thrust upon us by circumstances, people, or illness — can leave us depleted, wounded, or disconnected from the God who created us. In these moments of weariness and brokenness, we stand in need of **restoration**, **renewal**, and **realignment** with our Creator.

In this beautifully architected and God-inspired devotional collection, Stephanie Franklin-Suber gently but powerfully guides you through a sacred journey to restore your body, renew your soul, and realign your spirit.

Stephanie has walked this very path — from brokenness into wholeness through the transformative power of God's Word. God miraculously healed and delivered her from cancer, from years of chronic illness, and most recently from cardiac arrest. In each chapter of her testimony, God revealed to her the sacredness of her temple and showed her that, through faith in Jesus Christ, through Scripture, and by the work of the Holy Spirit, her temple could be rebuilt — God's way. Today, God has called Stephanie to help others rebuild their temples: body, soul, and spirit.

It is with joy and deep gratitude that I introduce you to this **Rebuild Your Temple, God's Way® Signature Faith and Health Collection**, which includes the three-book *10-Day Devotional Series* (*Restore Your Body, Renew Your Soul,* and *Realign Your Spirit*) and the two-book *30-Day Devotional Series* (the *30-Day Devotional* and the companion *Bible Study Workbook*).

As you embark on this sacred journey, do so with **anticipation** and **expectation**. Allow the Word of God to minister to your soul through Scripture and Reflection. Worship God with your body through the daily Temple Practice. Receive God's healing and restoration by engaging the Health Coaching Tips. And experience spiritual alignment as your spirit connects with the Spirit of God through prayer and journaling in the *Rebuild Your Temple, God's Way® Journal*.

It is my honor and delight to invite you to experience this transformational journey.
Come, and Rebuild Your Temple, God's Way®.

Yours in Christ,
Rev. Anna L. Grant-Borden
Senior Pastor, Mt. Airy Presbyterian Church
Philadelphia, Pennsylvania

Table of Contents

Daily Devotionals

Each day includes Scripture, Reflection, Temple Practice, Health Coaching Tip, Prayer, Journal Prompt, and Affirmation.

Part I – Restore Your Body

Part II – Renew Your Soul

Part III – Realign Your Spirit

Author's Introduction

This *Rebuild Your Temple, God's Way® Faith and Health 30-Day Devotional* was created to accompany the *Rebuild Your Temple, God's Way® Faith and Health Devotional Bible Study Workbook* and the *Rebuild Your Temple, God's Way® Journal* to guide you into a deeper, more personal encounter with the triune nature of God.

Your body is one of God's greatest gifts—a sacred Triune Human Temple™ (Body–Soul–Spirit) where His Holy Spirit dwells. When God gave King David the design for the Holy Temple in Jerusalem, it reflected His triune nature: Father, Son, and Holy Spirit. The Temple had three parts—the *Outer Court*, the *Inner Court*, and the *Holiest of Holies*—each representing a deeper place of worship and intimacy with Him.

You, too, were created in God's triune image as a Triune Human Temple™ (Body–Soul–Spirit). Your **body** personifies the *Outer Court*, where visible acts of stewardship and worship take place. The **soul**—your mind, will, and emotions—mirrors the *Inner Court*, where thoughts and desires are consecrated to Him. And your **spirit** embodies the *Holiest of Holies*, the inner sanctuary of communion with God.

The Triune Temple Journey™ structure of this *Devotional* and the *Bible Study Workbook* is modeled on the divine design of the Temple and the triune nature of God. It unites three progressively deeper journeys into your Triune Human Temple™ (Body–Soul–Spirit) into one 30-day rhythm:

- **Part I** – *Restore Your Body* (Days 1–10):
  Rebuild your *Outer Court* through nourishment, movement, and rest, honoring God the Father, by honoring your body.

- **Part II** – *Renew Your Soul* (Days 11–20):
  Enter your *Inner Court*, where God the Son, heals your emotional wounds and renews your mind with His peace.

- **Part III** – *Realign Your Spirit* (Days 21–30):
  Dwell in your *Holiest of Holies*, where God the Holy Spirit restores communion, brings your life into harmony with our triune God, and leads you into your God-given purpose.

These pages were born from my own story of *Rebuilding My Temple, God's Way®*—through cancer, chronic illness, and miraculous cardiac arrest—where God, in three persons, met me again and again with healing, hope, and restoration. The same God who restored me will meet you wherever you are in your faith and health journey and restore you too.

This is a sacred journey of rebuilding your temple—from the *Outer Court* to the

Inner Court to the *Holiest of Holies* for transformation from the outside in and the inside out.

As you move through each part—**Restore, Renew, and Realign**—you will rediscover what it means to live as the dwelling place of God: whole, healthy, and holy.

May this *Devotional,* the *Bible Study Workbook* and the *Journal* become your daily altar—a place of worship, wellness, and wonder—as you *Rebuild Your Temple, God's Way*®.

How to Use This Devotional

This *Devotional* was created to be used **side by side** with the *Rebuild Your Temple, God's Way® Faith and Health Bible Study Workbook*.

Each day in this *Devotional* corresponds directly with a day in the *Bible Study Workbook*—same title, Scripture, and theme—so that you can move from *inspiration* in this *Devotional* to *transformation* in the *Bible Study Workbook* through deeper study, reflection, and application.

You are encouraged to use the *Rebuild Your Temple, God's Way® Journal* or your own personal journal for more space to capture your prayers, insights, and breakthroughs in this *Devotional* and the *Bible Study Workbook*.

Each Daily Devotional includes seven devotional elements: Scripture, Reflection, Temple Practice, Health Coaching Tip, Prayer, Journal Prompt, and Affirmation.

Take one day at a time.

Scripture: Read the Scripture slowly and meditate on it to anchor your journey in the Word.

Reflection: Sit with the Reflection to gain deeper understanding of how and why our triune God cares about every aspect of your health and wholeness.

Temple Practice: Practice the simple step in Temple Practice to put stewardship of your holistic health in action and form holistic healthy habits.

Health Coaching Tip: Apply the Health Coaching Tip for ways to promote holistic health.

Prayer: Pray the Prayer aloud (if you can) for strength, encouragement and empowerment.

Journal Prompt: Write your response in your *Journal* to record your insights, discernment and progress through self-reflection.

Affirmation: Speak the Affirmation over your life to motivate you throughout each day.

As you move from **Restore** to **Renew** to **Realign**, may your body be strengthened by our Creator, may your soul be calmed by our Savior, and may your spirit be brought into harmony with the Holy Spirit.

May you enjoy and embrace this journey to *Rebuild Your Temple, God's Way®!*

Your 30-Day Triune Temple Journey™ At A Glance

Part	Restore Your Body	Renew Your Soul	Realign Your Spirit
Temple Sanctuary	Outer Court	Inner Court	Holiest of Holies
Triune Divine Person	God the Father	God the Son	God the Holy Spirit
Triune Human Temple™	Body	Soul	Spirit
Spiritual Focus	Worship through action	Worship through surrender	Worship through communion
Result	Strengthened stewardship and gratitude	Inner healing and renewed peace	Alignment and divine purpose

As you move through this Triune Temple Journey™, you will experience the beauty of transformation from the outside in and the inside out—restored in body, renewed in soul, and realigned in spirit.

May every page lead you deeper into the presence of the One who created you, redeemed you, and now dwells within you.

PART I – RESTORE YOUR BODY

A 10-Day Journey to Physical Health and Wholeness

Rebuild the *Outer Court* of your temple through
nourishment, movement, and rest.

RESTORE

Restore Your Body. Renew Your Soul. Realign Your Spirit.™

 DAY 1 – YOUR BODY IS A TEMPLE

Scripture
Do you not know that your bodies are temples of the Holy Spirit, who is in you, whom you have received from God? You are not your own; you were bought at a price. Therefore honor God with your bodies.
(1 Corinthians 6:19–20 NIV)

Reflection
Paul wrote these words to believers in Corinth, a culture that treated the body as something to indulge or ignore. He reminded them that redemption makes the body sacred—it now belongs to the Lord who purchased it.

Your body, like the *Outer Court* of God's Temple, is where your daily worship begins. Caring for your physical health is not vanity; it is stewardship. Each nourishing choice, each moment of rest, each step taken in gratitude becomes a form of worship that honors the God who dwells within you. When you view your body as His dwelling, self-care transforms from duty to devotion.

Today, invite your Creator to show you one area—nutrition, hydration, movement, breathing, or rest—where He wants to restore reverence.

Temple Practice
Choose one gentle action today that blesses your body—walk, stretch, breathe, sip water slowly, or rest intentionally—and thank God with each choice and action.

Health Coaching Tip
Start with small, simple steps to honor your body as God's entrusted gift. Consistency matters more than intensity. Faithful repetition transforms simple acts into lasting habits of stewardship and care.

Prayer
Heavenly Father,
Thank You for creating my body as Your temple. Teach me to honor You through how I care for it today.
In Jesus' name, I pray, Amen.

Journal Prompt
What would change if you treated your body as a sacred space of worship?

Affirmation
I honor God by honoring my temple through every choice I make.

 DAY 2 – NOURISH YOUR TEMPLE

Scripture
So whether you eat or drink or whatever you do, do it all for the glory of God.
(1 Corinthians 10:31 NIV)

Reflection
From the manna in the wilderness to the loaves and fishes that fed the multitude, Scripture shows God's concern for daily bread. Every meal is His reminder that He provides what sustains both body and soul. When you eat with gratitude, ordinary nourishment becomes sacred fellowship.

Paul's instruction to the Corinthians calls you to shift your focus from self to glory: eating and drinking become opportunities to magnify the Giver.

Invite God to the table. Slow your pace; notice texture, color, and flavor; receive each bite as grace. Healthy eating is not restriction—it is agreement with the Lord's desire for your flourishing.

Temple Practice
Pause before eating today. Pray a short blessing and take your first three bites slowly, thanking God for flavor, texture, and strength.

Health Coaching Tip
Plan balanced meals with lean protein, colorful produce, and whole grains. Mindful eating improves digestion and satisfaction.

Prayer
Heavenly Father,
Thank You for the gift of food that nourishes my body and reflects Your goodness.
Help me to eat with mindfulness and gratitude.
In Jesus' name, I pray, Amen.

Journal Prompt
How can mealtime become an act of worship in your daily rhythm?

Affirmation
I take every bite with gratitude to honor the God who sustains me.

# DAY 3 – HYDRATE AND REFRESH

Scripture

The Lord will guide you always; He will satisfy your needs in a sun-scorched land and will strengthen your frame. You will be like a well-watered garden, like a spring whose waters never fail.
(Isaiah 58:11 NIV)

Reflection

In Isaiah's promise to a weary people, God likens His care to water flowing through dry ground. Just as the earth thirsts for rain, our bodies long for refreshment. Water is one of the simplest yet most profound reminders of His provision—it cleanses, cools, and sustains every system He designed.

When you pause to drink, remember the Living Water who never fails. Hydration becomes worship when it turns your thoughts toward dependence on Him. Let each sip remind you that He strengthens your frame and refreshes your purpose.

Temple Practice

Drink a full glass of water before each meal today, thanking God for the refreshment of His presence.

Health Coaching Tip

Aim for eight cups of water daily. Keep a refillable bottle nearby and infuse with fruit or herbs for variety.

Prayer

Heavenly Father,
Please refresh my body. Quench my thirst with Your provision and renew my strength for the work ahead.
In Jesus' name, I pray, Amen.

Journal Prompt

How does physical refreshment remind you of God's continual renewal?

Affirmation

I am refreshed by the Living Water and strengthened to flourish.

 DAY 4 – MOVE WITH GRACE

Scripture
For in Him we live and move and have our being.
(Acts 17:28 NIV)

Reflection
Paul's declaration in Athens grounds all movement in divine origin. Every heartbeat and step are evidence of God's sustaining power. He designed motion not just for function, but for joy.

When you move your body, you participate in His creative rhythm.

In the *Outer Court* of the Temple in Jerusalem, priests served through continual motion—lifting, carrying, preparing offerings. Their labor was worship. Your daily movement can carry the same intention. Whether you stretch, walk, or exercise, do it as prayer in motion. Graceful movement honors the One who gives breath and energy, reminding you that strength and coordination are gifts to steward, not possessions to boast in.

Temple Practice
Take a brisk walk or gentle stretch while thanking God for the ability to move and serve Him.

Health Coaching Tip
Consistent movement improves circulation, joint health, and mood. Find activities you enjoy—walking, dancing, gardening—to keep it sustainable.

Prayer
Creator God,
Thank You for the gift of movement. Help me to use my strength to praise and serve You with joy and grace.
In Jesus' name, I pray, Amen.

Journal Prompt
How can you turn everyday movement into worship?

Affirmation
I live, move, and have my being in God, and my motion is worship.

 DAY 5 – BREATHE AND RELEASE

Scripture
Then the Lord God formed a man from the dust of the ground and breathed into his nostrils the breath of life, and the man became a living being.
(Genesis 2:7 NIV)

Reflection
Life began with God's breath. That same divine rhythm continues in you—inhale grace, exhale surrender. Each breath is both miracle and message: you live because He gives. When anxiety constricts your breathing, remember that peace is only one deep inhale away.

The Hebrew word for "breath," *ruach,* also means "spirit." Breathing slowly and intentionally reconnects you with the One who animates your being. In those moments, stress yields to presence, and fear gives way to faith. Let today's breathing become a holy conversation—receiving His Spirit, releasing your burdens.

Temple Practice
Pause three times today to take five slow, deep breaths. Inhale God's peace; exhale every care.

Health Coaching Tip
Deep breathing lowers stress hormones and steadies heart rate. Practice before meals or bedtime for calm and clarity.

Prayer
Creator God,
I praise You for breathing Your life into my body. Help me to calm my nervous system by releasing tension so that I can rest in Your presence.
In Jesus' name, I pray, Amen.

Journal Prompt
What do you need to exhale and surrender to God today?

Affirmation
I receive God's peace and release my burdens with each breath I take.

 DAY 6 – BE STILL AND KNOW HIM

Scripture

Be still, and know that I am God; I will be exalted among the nations, I will be exalted in the earth.

(Psalm 46:10 NIV)

Reflection

The psalmist wrote these words in the middle of chaos—nations raging, mountains trembling, waters roaring. God's command was not for inactivity but for trust: *Be still.* In stillness, you remember that the world turns by His hand, not yours. Stress and anxiety often drive you to over-function; quietness recenters you on the sufficiency of God the Father.

When you practice stillness, you enter the inner sanctuary of peace even while tending to your outer-court body. A few minutes of silence can reset your heartbeat and renew your mind. It is in the quiet that you hear His gentle whisper reminding you, "I am God, and I am with you."

Temple Practice

Sit in silence today for five minutes. Focus on slow breathing and repeat, "You are God, and I trust You."

Health Coaching Tip

Intentional quiet lowers blood pressure and cortisol. Unplug from screens daily and let your body experience calm.

Prayer

Almighty God,

Teach me to be still in Your presence. Under the shadow of Your wings, I am safe and protected. Quiet my racing thoughts so I may know You more deeply.

In Jesus' name, I pray, Amen.

Journal Prompt

What distractions keep you from being still before God?

Affirmation

I find God's strength and peace in stillness.

 DAY 7 – REST TO REBUILD

Scripture
In vain you rise early and stay up late, toiling for food to eat—for He grants sleep to those He loves.
(Psalm 127:2 NIV)

Reflection
The builder who never sleeps eventually weakens his foundation. God created night and day so that work and rest would partner together. Sleep is not wasted time—it is sacred rebuilding.

While you rest, God repairs tissues, restores hormones, and renews energy for purpose. The body you steward needs this rhythm to thrive.

Israel's farmers practiced Sabbath rest to trust God with provision; your nightly rest is a smaller Sabbath of faith. When you lie down, you declare that God is working even when you are not.

Let each evening become an altar where you lay down your labor and receive His rest. As your body regains strength, may it serve as a vessel for God's good work.

Temple Practice
Turn off electronics 30 minutes before bed. Dim the lights, breathe deeply, and thank God for His faithful protection while you sleep.

Health Coaching Tip
Aim for 7–8 hours of sleep. A dark, cool room and a consistent bedtime support hormone balance and recovery.

Prayer
Most High God,
Thank You for rest that restores. Help me to trust that You are working all things together for my good and that You are healing and restoring my body all through the night.
In Jesus' name, I pray, Amen.

Journal Prompt
How does trusting God change the way you approach sleep and rest?

Affirmation
I receive God's gift of rest and awake restored.

 # DAY 8 – LISTEN TO YOUR BODY

Scripture

Then he lay down under the bush and fell asleep. All at once an angel touched him and said, "Get up and eat." He looked around, and there by his head was some bread baked over hot coals, and a jar of water.
(1 Kings 19:5–6 NIV)

Reflection

After Elijah's great victory came exhaustion and despair. God's response was practical: sleep, food, and water. The Lord cared for Elijah's physical needs before speaking to his heart. In the same way, your body's signals—fatigue, hunger, tension—are invitations from God to slow down and receive care. Listening is holy stewardship.

When you ignore your body, you silence one of God's messengers. When you respond with compassion, you align with His design. God does not condemn your limitations; He meets you in them.

Temple Practice

Check in with your body three times today. Ask, "What do I need right now—rest, nourishment, or movement?"

Health Coaching Tip

Regular body awareness prevents burnout. Gentle stretching, hydration, and balanced meals keep energy steady.

Prayer

Lord of Lords,
Thank You for creating my body with wisdom. Help me listen and respond with kindness and gratitude.
In Jesus' name, I pray, Amen.

Journal Prompt

What message is your body sending you today, and how will you respond?

Affirmation

I am fearfully and wonderfully made; I listen to my body with grace.

 DAY 9 – RENEW YOUR STRENGTH

Scripture

But those who hope in the Lord will renew their strength. They will soar on wings like eagles; they will run and not grow weary, they will walk and not be faint.
(Isaiah 40:31 NIV)

Reflection

Isaiah spoke to a weary nation in exile, reminding them that hope—not human effort—renews strength. God promises endurance for those who wait on Him. Physical strength mirrors spiritual truth: energy flows from the Source.

When you nourish your body, hydrate, and move, you participate in the renewal He provides. Stewardship of health prepares you for Kingdom purpose. Renewal happens when you exchange exhaustion for empowerment. Waiting on God is not idle—it is aligning your rhythms with His.

As you care for your body, He multiplies your stamina to serve.

Temple Practice

Take a short walk or do a gentle stretch while praying Isaiah 40:31. Feel His promise strengthening your steps.

Health Coaching Tip

Balanced meals, hydration, and consistent movement maintain energy. Ten minutes outdoors can reset body and mind.

Prayer

Father,
Thank You for renewing my strength. Help me to wait patiently as You heal my body. Teach me to care for my body with wisdom and gratitude.
In Jesus' name, I pray, Amen.

Journal Prompt

Where do you need to exchange weariness for God's renewing strength?

Affirmation

I wait on the Lord, and He renews my strength daily for His purpose.

 DAY 10 – CELEBRATE YOUR PROGRESS

Scripture
Being confident of this, that He who began a good work in you will carry it on to completion until the day of Christ Jesus.
(Philippians 1:6 NIV)

Reflection
Your faith and health journey is one of progress, not perfection. Paul's words remind you that God Himself is the finisher of the work He begins. Each small change—one more glass of water, one mindful meal, one restful night—is evidence of His grace in action. Celebrate your progress because celebration fuels perseverance. Gratitude shifts your focus from what remains undone to what God has already restored.

When you rejoice in every small step, you acknowledge that stewardship of your health is a journey of partnership with Him. The One who created you and began your healing will carry it to completion in His perfect timing.

Temple Practice
Write down three areas of progress from these ten days. Thank God for His faithfulness in each.

Health Coaching Tip
Celebrate wins with non-food rewards—time outdoors, music, or a relaxing bath—to reinforce healthy patterns.

Prayer
Lord,
I am grateful to You for the good work You have begun in me. Teach me to celebrate progress and trust Your process.
In Jesus' name, I pray, Amen.

Journal Prompt
How will you continue to celebrate and sustain your progress with God?

Affirmation
I rejoice in every step God helps me take toward health and wholeness.

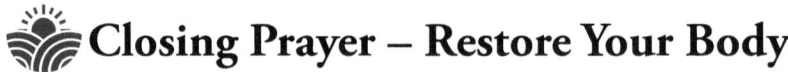 Closing Prayer – Restore Your Body

Heavenly Father,

Thank You for meeting me in this sacred journey of restoration.
You have reminded me that my body is Your temple—
a vessel of worship, not of striving; a dwelling of grace, not of guilt.

As I continue to rebuild my temple,
teach me to see every healthy choice as an act of faith.
May nourishment, rest, and movement become offerings of love to You.
Please continue to guide my steps, breathe Your breath of life into my lungs,
and strengthen my hands for the restoration work You have called me to do.

Thank You for healing what was physically broken
and restoring what seemed beyond repair.
Help me walk in courage and confidence, knowing that You who began this good
work in me will carry it to completion.

I dedicate this restored body—Your temple—back to You,
for Your service, Your glory, and Your purpose.

In Jesus' name, I pray, Amen.

PART II – RENEW YOUR SOUL

A 10-Day Journey to Emotional Health and Mindset Renewal

Rebuild the *Inner Court* of your temple through
surrender, gratitude, and peace.

RENEW

Restore Your Body. Renew Your Soul. Realign Your Spirit.™

# DAY 11 – GUARD YOUR HEART

Scripture
Above all else, guard your heart, for everything you do flows from it.
(Proverbs 4:23 NIV)

Reflection
The heart, in Scripture, represents your whole inner life—your thoughts, feelings, and will. Solomon's command to "guard your heart" is not about building walls but about cultivating awareness. Your heart is sacred ground where God the Son plants truth, but it can also become cluttered by fear, doubt, and distraction.

Guarding your heart means watching what influences your emotions and thoughts. It means choosing what to dwell on, who to trust, and what to release. When you bring every feeling—joy, worry, or pain—before the Son, you invite His peace to protect you. The more you surrender your emotions to Him, the more your heart becomes a place where His love freely flows.

Temple Practice
Pause today and ask, "What has been shaping my emotions lately—the truth of the Living Word or the world's noise?" Offer one burden to Him in prayer.

Health Coaching Tip
Limit emotional overload. Step away from social media or news for a set time each day. Quiet space nurtures emotional clarity.

Prayer
Lord Jesus,
Help me guard my heart with Your wisdom. Protect my thoughts and emotions so Your peace can flow freely within me.
In Your name, I pray, Amen.

Journal Prompt
What does your heart need protection from today, and how can you guard it through prayer and boundaries?

Affirmation
I guard the sacred ground of my heart with the love of Christ. Everything I do flows from it.

 DAY 12 – RENEW YOUR MIND

Scripture
Do not conform to the pattern of this world, but be transformed by the renewing of your mind.
(Romans 12:2 NIV)

Reflection
Paul reminds us that transformation begins in the mind. The world trains you to react with fear, comparison, and self-criticism, but Christ calls you to think differently. Renewal happens when you invite the Living Word to reshape your thoughts and replace lies with truth.

Your mind can be a battlefield, but it can also become a sanctuary. Every time you choose gratitude over grumbling or faith over fear, you strengthen new pathways of peace. Meditating on the Word literally re-patterns your brain, restoring your capacity for joy and resilience.

Healing the soul begins with this surrender: "Lord, change how I think so I can live as You see me."

Temple Practice
Write down one negative thought you have been repeating. Cross it out and replace it with a promise from Scripture.

Health Coaching Tip
Feed your mind as carefully as your body. Start or end each day with uplifting music, Scripture reading, or journaling.

Prayer
Lord Jesus,
Please renew my mind with Your truth. Transform my thoughts so they reflect Your mind of peace and power.
In Your name, I pray, Amen.

Journal Prompt
What thought patterns need to change for your mind to align with the truth of the Living Word?

Affirmation
I renew my mind daily by the truth of the Living Word.

# DAY 13 – LAY IT DOWN

Scripture

Cast your cares on the Lord and He will sustain you; He will never let the righteous be shaken.
(Psalm 55:22 NIV)

Reflection

David wrote this psalm in a season of betrayal and emotional pain. His words remind us that God the Son, not only hears our cries—He carries them. To "cast" your cares is to throw them onto His shoulders, trusting His strength to sustain what yours cannot. Emotional burdens—fear, guilt, grief, or disappointment—were never meant to be permanent cargo.

When you hold onto pain, it begins to hold onto you. But when you lay it down before the Lord, you make space for peace to enter. Jesus Christ never promised a life without sorrow, but He did promise His sustaining presence in every storm. Lay down your worries, your regrets, and your what-ifs.

His hands are strong enough to hold them—and gentle enough to heal them.

Temple Practice

Find a quiet space. Write your heaviest concern on paper, then fold it and pray, "Lord, I cast this care on You."

Health Coaching Tip

Chronic stress tightens muscles and drains energy. Stretch slowly while breathing deeply, releasing both physical and emotional tension.

Prayer

Lord Jesus,
I lay down my cares before You. Sustain me with Your strength and fill my soul with Your peace.
In Your name, I pray, Amen.

Journal Prompt

What burden have you been carrying alone that you can entrust to Jesus today?

Affirmation

I cast my cares on the Lord. He sustains me with unfailing peace.

 DAY 14 – OVERCOME YOUR FEAR

Scripture

So do not fear, for I am with you; do not be dismayed, for I am your God. I will strengthen you and help you; I will uphold you with my righteous right hand.
(Isaiah 41:10 NIV)

Reflection

Fear is a natural response—but left unchecked, it becomes a barrier to peace. Jesus Christ never condemns you for feeling fear; instead, He invites you to transform it into trust. Each "Do not fear" in Scripture is paired with a reason: "for I am with you." The presence of God the Son, is the antidote to fear.

Sometimes fear rises from real wounds or trauma. The limbic system—the body's alarm center—remembers pain and keeps you on high alert. Yet even here, God the Son speaks calm into chaos. As you breathe deeply and speak His promises, you train both your brain and your spirit to rest in His safety. Perfect love really does cast out fear.

Temple Practice

Pause and whisper, "Jesus, You are with me," when fear surfaces. Visualize His hand steadying your heart.

Health Coaching Tip

Ground yourself in the present moment. Feel your feet on the floor, take three slow breaths, and focus on one truth: "I am safe in Christ's care."

Prayer

Savior,
Thank You that Your presence drives out fear. Calm my anxious heart and fill me with Your perfect peace.
In Your name, I pray, Amen.

Journal Prompt

What fear has been keeping you from peace, and how can you invite Jesus into it today?

Affirmation

I will not fear, for Jesus is with me—strengthening and upholding me.

 # DAY 15 – CHOOSE PEACE

Scripture
Do not be anxious about anything, but in every situation, by prayer and petition, with thanksgiving, present your requests to God. And the peace of God, which transcends all understanding, will guard your hearts and your minds in Christ Jesus.
(Philippians 4:6–7 NIV)

Reflection
Anxiety is what happens when the soul forgets that Christ Jesus is near. Paul's words are not a command to suppress worry but an invitation to redirect it—to turn anxiety into prayer. When you express your concerns to God the Son, with gratitude, you exchange chaos for calm.

Peace is not the absence of trouble; it is the presence of Christ within it. Like a guard at the city gate, His peace surrounds your heart and mind, protecting you from fear's return. Each time you choose prayer over panic, you strengthen your trust that He truly is in control.

Temple Practice
Pause and say, "Lord, I give this to You," when anxiety arises. Then, name three things you are grateful for in this moment.

Health Coaching Tip
Establish a "peace ritual." Brew tea, light a candle, or play worship music during prayer to calm your heart and mind.

Prayer
Redeemer,
I am grateful that Your peace guards my heart and mind. Teach me to turn every worry into prayer and worship.
In Your name, I pray, Amen.

Journal Prompt
How does gratitude shift your thoughts and emotions when you feel anxious?

Affirmation
I guard my heart and mind in the peace of Christ Jesus.

 DAY 16 – REST IN HIS GRACE

Scripture

He does not treat us as our sins deserve or repay us according to our iniquities. For as high as the heavens are above the earth, so great is His love for those who fear Him; as far as the east is from the west, so far has He removed our transgressions from us.
(Psalm 103:10–12 NIV)

Reflection

Shame is one of the heaviest emotions the soul can carry. It whispers, "You are still defined by what you did." But God's grace answers, "You are defined by what My Son has done." David's psalm reminds us that divine forgiveness is not partial—it is complete. The blood of the Lamb removes guilt thoroughly—east and west can never meet again.

When you rehearse regret, you reopen wounds Christ already healed. Resting in grace means believing His mercy outweighs your mistakes. Let His compassion quiet the voice of condemnation until only love remains.

Temple Practice

Visualize laying your regrets at the foot of the cross. As you breathe out, whisper, "I release this to Your grace."

Health Coaching Tip

Self-compassion supports a healthy mind. When guilt arises, practice slow, diaphragmatic breathing to calm your nervous system and remind yourself: "I am forgiven and loved."

Prayer

Redeemer,
Thank You for Your mercy that covers all my failures. Teach me to rest—not strive—in Your grace.
In Your name, I pray, Amen.

Journal Prompt

What past mistake or regret is God inviting you to release into His grace?

Affirmation

I rest in the unchanging grace of Christ. His blood has washed away my guilt and shame.

DAY 17 – REFRAME THE STORM

Scripture
Consider it pure joy, my brothers and sisters, whenever you face trials of many kinds, because you know that the testing of your faith produces perseverance. Let perseverance finish its work so that you may be mature and complete, not lacking anything.
(James 1:2–4 NIV)

Reflection
Life's storms can feel like punishment, yet James reveals they are invitations to growth. Trials expose what is fragile so Jesus can strengthen what is lasting. Reframing a storm does not deny pain; it recognizes purpose.

When you view difficulty through faith's lens, hope begins to surface. Each challenge can develop patience, empathy, and endurance—the spiritual muscles of maturity. Even emotional storms—grief, disappointment, anxiety—become classrooms where the grace of Christ teaches trust. The same wind that bends the tree also deepens its roots.

Temple Practice
Recall one current challenge. Ask Jesus to reveal your weakness and what He is trying to teach you through the trial.

Health Coaching Tip
Stress reframed as "growth energy" changes the body's chemistry. During tense moments, repeat, "This is hard, but it is helping me grow," to shift from panic to purpose.

Prayer
Wonderful Counselor,
Help me see my trials through Your eyes. Strengthen my faith until endurance finishes its good work.
In Your name, I pray, Amen.

Journal Prompt
How might your present storm be shaping Christlike character within you?

Affirmation
I have deep roots of faith in Christ. My resilience is strengthened by every storm.

 DAY 18 – HEAL YOUR BROKEN HEART

Scripture
He heals the brokenhearted and binds up their wounds.
(Psalm 147:3 NIV)

Reflection
Grief changes you; it does not have to destroy you. Jesus is always with you. He never rushes your sorrow—He sits with you in it. The Hebrew image of this verse is intimate: God the Son personally binds the torn places of the heart like a skilled physician. Every tear invites His tender presence.

Emotional healing takes time and trust. When pain resurfaces, let it become prayer rather than isolation. God's comfort is not abstract—it comes through His Son, His Word, and often through compassionate people. In His hands, your heartbreak becomes holy ground where new compassion grows.

Temple Practice
Write a letter to Jesus about your loss or disappointment. End it with gratitude for His presence in your healing.

Health Coaching Tip
Crying is the body's cleansing mechanism. Welcome tears—they release stress hormones and promote calm. Pair tears with hydration and rest.

Prayer
Healer of Hearts,
By Your stripes, I am healed. Thank You for binding my wounds. Hold me close as You turn my pain into purpose.
In Your name, I pray, Amen.

Journal Prompt
Where do you still feel broken, and how has Christ already begun to mend you?

Affirmation
Jesus heals my broken heart and restores joy to my soul.

 # DAY 19 – CULTIVATE JOY

Scripture
Do not grieve, for the joy of the Lord is your strength.
(Nehemiah 8:10 NIV)

Reflection
Joy is not the denial of pain but the discovery of God's presence within it. When the Israelites heard God's law after exile, they wept—but Nehemiah reminded them that celebration, not shame, was their strength. Gratitude opens the door to that same holy joy today.

Each act of thanksgiving—no matter how small—shifts your focus from loss to abundance. Joy does not always shout; sometimes it whispers through sunlight, laughter, or the quiet assurance that God is still good. He gave you His only Son. As you cultivate gratitude, you till the soil of your soul for joy to take root and grow strong.

Temple Practice
List five things—simple or profound—for which you are thankful. Read them aloud as praise.

Health Coaching Tip
Daily gratitude journaling lowers stress and improves sleep. Before bed, record three blessings to train your brain toward positivity.

Prayer
Lord Jesus,
Plant deep joy in my heart. Let gratitude be the song that strengthens me each day.
In Your name, I pray, Amen.

Journal Prompt
How has gratitude changed your emotional outlook recently?

Affirmation
I am grateful for the goodness of Christ, and the joy of the Lord is my strength.

DAY 20 – WALK IN FREEDOM

Scripture
So if the Son sets you free, you will be free indeed.
(John 8:36 NIV)

Reflection
Freedom is more than the absence of bondage—it is the presence of peace. When Jesus spoke these words, He offered liberation not only from sin but from fear, guilt, and every lie that imprisons the mind. Emotional freedom begins when you believe His truth over your trauma.

God the Son does not erase your story; He redeems it. The memories that once triggered pain can become testimonies of grace. Walking in freedom means choosing faith daily. It means releasing what no longer defines you and embracing the identity Christ secured for you. You are no longer captive to the past; you are a temple filled with His light.

Temple Practice
Take a short walk outdoors. With each step, thank Jesus for one area of freedom He has given you.

Health Coaching Tip
Movement reinforces empowerment. A brisk 10-minute walk boosts mood and confidence—physical reminders of inner liberty.

Prayer
Lamb of God,
Thank You for setting me free. Help me live each day in Your peace and the confidence of Your truth.
In Your name, I pray, Amen.

Journal Prompt
Where have you seen evidence of Christ's freedom in your emotional life?

Affirmation
I walk in peace, confidence, and joy. The Son has set me free.

 Closing Prayer – Renew Your Soul

Lord Jesus,

Thank You for leading me through this journey of soul renewal.
You have quieted my anxious thoughts, healed my wounds, and filled the broken places of my heart with peace.

As I continue to guard my heart and renew my mind,
teach me to live from a place of trust rather than fear,
gratitude rather than worry,
and grace rather than guilt.

May You, as the Living Word, continue to transform my thoughts,
reshape my emotions,
and restore my will to align with Yours.
Let my soul be a sanctuary where Your peace reigns.

Thank You for the comfort that calms my storms,
the joy that strengthens me,
and the truth that sets me free.
Renew my soul daily with Your presence,
and let my life reflect the beauty of Your renewal.

In Your name, I pray, Amen.

PART III – REALIGN YOUR SPIRIT

A 10-Day Journey to Spiritual Health and Wholeness

Enter your *Holiest of Holies* — where the Holy Spirit restores communion, harmony, and purpose.

REALIGN

Restore Your Body. Renew Your Soul. Realign Your Spirit.™

 DAY 21 – DWELL IN HIS PRESENCE

Scripture
The Lord is close to the brokenhearted and saves those who are crushed in spirit.
(Psalm 34:18 NIV)

Reflection
When the spirit is weary, even prayer can feel heavy. Silence may echo louder than the voice of God's Holy Spirit, and worship may feel distant. Yet this is where healing begins—in the quiet, not the noise.

Jesus Christ does not stand apart from your brokenness; He draws near to it. He does not scold you for feeling dry; He sits beside you in it. He gave you His Holy Spirit to comfort you.

Spiritual dryness is not the absence of faith—it is an invitation to return to dependence on the Holy Spirit. Nearness to the Spirit is not earned through effort; it is received through openness. When you simply sit before Him—no words, no performance—you begin to sense His steady presence again.

The Spirit breathes where there has been no breath, rekindling the flame that suffering tried to extinguish. The same Spirit who breathed life into creation now breathes peace into your soul.

Temple Practice
Find a quiet place. Sit still for five minutes and whisper, "Holy Spirit, I know You are near." Breathe slowly as you rest in that truth.

Health Coaching Tip
Stillness restores spiritual rhythm and lowers stress. Schedule a daily "pause moment" to breathe, release tension, and welcome the Holy Spirit's peace.

Prayer
Holy Spirit,
Draw near to my crushed spirit. Help me rest in Your presence until my heart feels Your peace again.
In Jesus' name, I pray, Amen.

Journal Prompt
When have you felt most aware of the Holy Spirit's presence in difficult times?

Affirmation
I am sustained by the Holy Spirit in me, even in my brokenness. He is as close as the breath I breathe.

 DAY 22 – ABIDE IN THE VINE

Scripture
Remain in me, as I also remain in you. No branch can bear fruit by itself; it must remain in the vine.
(John 15:4–5 NIV)

Reflection
Spiritual dryness often comes when we try to live disconnected from the Source. Like a branch separated from the vine, our strength fades when we rely on self-effort.

Abiding is not striving—it is surrendering. It means resting in the truth that God's Spirit flows continually, even when you cannot feel it. Your role is to stay connected. Every act of prayer, worship, or quiet trust allows His life to flow again.

Over time, you will notice renewal—not forced growth, but gentle fruit born from communion. In abiding, your crushed spirit becomes a living branch again, nourished by divine love.

Temple Practice
Visualize your heart as a branch connected to Christ the Vine. With each breath, imagine His life-giving Spirit flowing into you.

Health Coaching Tip
Stay hydrated. Water mirrors the Spirit's renewing flow. As you drink, thank the Holy Spirit for sustaining your body, soul, and spirit.

Prayer
Holy Spirit,
Help me remain in You when I feel weak or dry. Let Your life flow through me and make me fruitful again.
In Jesus' name, I pray, Amen.

Journal Prompt
Where in your spiritual life have you been striving instead of abiding?

Affirmation
I remain connected to Christ, and His Spirit renews my strength.

 DAY 23 – WALK BY THE SPIRIT

Scripture
Since we live by the Spirit, let us keep in step with the Spirit.
(Galatians 5:25 NIV)

Reflection
Realignment begins when you stop forcing your own rhythm and start walking in the Spirit's. After trauma or hardship, it is easy to become spiritually out of sync—rushing ahead or lagging behind in fear or fatigue. The Spirit invites you to walk, not run; to move, not drift.

When you walk by the Spirit, you let His timing become yours. Each step is guided by grace, not guilt. Some days, your pace will be slow—but even slow steps toward intimacy with the Spirit are sacred. The goal is not perfection; it is presence.

As you walk in step with the Spirit, you will find He restores balance where chaos once ruled and purpose where confusion lingered.

Temple Practice
Take a mindful walk. Match your breathing to your steps. With each exhale, whisper, "Holy Spirit, guide me."

Health Coaching Tip
Walking outdoors enhances mood and spiritual focus. Ten minutes of movement can clear mental fog and open your heart to prayer.

Prayer
Holy Spirit,
Align my pace with Yours. Teach me to walk in harmony with Your guidance every day.
In Jesus' name, I pray, Amen.

Journal Prompt
What does "keeping in step with the Spirit" look like in this season of your life?

Affirmation
I walk in rhythm with the Spirit, guided by His peace and purpose.

 DAY 24 – ALIGN WITH HIS WORD

Scripture
Your word is a lamp for my feet, a light on my path.
(Psalm 119:105 NIV)

Reflection
In seasons of spiritual dryness, feelings cannot always be trusted, but the Word always can. Scripture steadies you when emotions waver and lights your path when darkness lingers.

The Word realigns your spirit because it reveals God's triune character. Reading the Bible is not just study—it is encounter. Each verse is a window through which His Spirit shines. When your mind is weary and your hope dim, open His Word as you would open a window to fresh air.

Let truth illuminate your confusion until peace returns to your spirit.

Temple Practice
Read Psalm 119:105 aloud. Then, write it in your journal, adding a short prayer: "Holy Spirit, align my steps with the Word today."

Health Coaching Tip
Morning Scripture reading before checking messages reduces stress and sets a positive mindset for the day.

Prayer
Holy Spirit,
Guide me and let Your Word light my path and anchor my thoughts in truth.
In Jesus' name, I pray, Amen.

Journal Prompt
How has Scripture recently corrected or comforted your spirit?

Affirmation
I am filled with the Holy Spirit who shines in me, lights my path, and aligns my spirit with His truth.

 DAY 25 – LISTEN FOR HIS VOICE

Scripture
My sheep listen to my voice; I know them, and they follow me.
(John 10:27 NIV)

Reflection
When life feels noisy, discerning the voice of the Holy Spirit can seem impossible. But His voice is not lost—it is simply waiting for space. The Holy Spirit often whispers, not because He is distant, but because He desires closeness.

To hear Him again, quiet the inner clutter of worry and distraction. The more you rest, the clearer His presence becomes. His voice is peace, not pressure; assurance, not accusation.

When your spirit learns to listen, you will realize He never stopped speaking—you just stopped hearing. Reconnection begins not with louder prayers, but with quieter hearts.

Temple Practice
Find a peaceful spot. Take three slow breaths. Whisper, "Speak, Holy Spirit. Your servant is listening." Wait in silence for one minute.

Health Coaching Tip
Noise fatigue increases stress hormones. Take short "sound fasts" throughout your day to rest your senses and attune your spirit.

Prayer
Holy Spirit,
Tune my ears to Your voice and quiet the noise within me. I long to hear and follow You closely.
In Jesus' name, I pray, Amen.

Journal Prompt
When was the last time you sensed the Holy Spirit speaking to your spirit?

Affirmation
I quiet and open my spirit. I hear the Holy Spirit's voice with peace and clarity.

❤️ DAY 26 – WORSHIP IN SPIRIT AND TRUTH

Scripture
Yet a time is coming and has now come when the true worshipers will worship the Father in the Spirit and in truth, for they are the kind of worshipers the Father seeks.
(John 4:23–24 NIV)

Reflection
Worship is not a performance; it is participation in the life of the Spirit. When Jesus spoke these words to the Samaritan woman, He revealed that worship no longer depends on a temple built by hands—the Holy Spirit has made your spirit His dwelling place.

True worship happens when spirit meets Spirit: honesty replaces striving, surrender replaces routine. In pain or in praise, worship reconnects you to the God who never left. As you open your spirit to Him, the Spirit shifts your perspective, restoring joy where sorrow lingered.

Temple Practice
Play a worship song that draws you near to the Holy Spirit. As you sing or listen, focus on His presence rather than your performance.

Health Coaching Tip
Singing slows the breath and lowers stress. Hum or sing softly to steady your heartbeat and invite calm.

Prayer
Holy Spirit,
Teach me to worship beyond words—in truth, humility, and gratitude.
In Jesus' name, I pray, Amen.

Journal Prompt
How does authentic worship renew your sense of connection with the Holy Spirit?

Affirmation
I worship in my spirit and in truth. The presence of the Holy Spirit fills my spirit with peace.

DAY 27 – PRAY WITHOUT CEASING

Scripture
Rejoice always, pray continually, give thanks in all circumstances; for this is God's will for you in Christ Jesus.
(1 Thessalonians 5:16–18 NIV)

Reflection
Continuous prayer is not endless talking—it is unbroken awareness of God. The Spirit turns ordinary moments into sacred dialogue: a breath becomes thanksgiving; a sigh becomes surrender.

When you let the Spirit guide your thoughts, prayer becomes as natural as breathing. The conversation never stops; it simply flows beneath the surface of your day. In that communion, dryness fades. You rediscover that prayer is not something you do to reach God—it is what happens when you walk with Him.

Temple Practice
Pause three times today to whisper a simple prayer: "Thank You, Holy Spirit." "Help me, Holy Spirit." "I love You, Holy Spirit."

Health Coaching Tip
Pair breath with prayer. Inhale— "Holy Spirit, You are here." Exhale— "I rest in Your peace."

Prayer
Holy Spirit,
Breathe prayer through me today. Keep my spirit tuned to Your constant presence.
In Jesus' name, I pray, Amen.

Journal Prompt
What everyday activities could become prayer when done with awareness of the Holy Spirit?

Affirmation
I walk in constant conversation with the Holy Spirit. Prayer is the rhythm of my spirit.

 DAY 28 – SURRENDER YOUR WILL

Scripture
Father, if You are willing, take this cup from Me; yet not My will, but Yours be done.
(Luke 22:42 NIV)

Reflection
Surrender is not loss—it is alignment. Jesus' prayer in Gethsemane reveals holy strength: choosing trust when every emotion resists. The Holy Spirit helps you pray the same way—translating your sighs into surrender.

When life feels uncertain, your spirit clings to control, but peace grows only where will yields to wisdom. To surrender is to rest in the love of God—the Father, the Son, and the Holy Spirit—knowing He chooses what refines, not what destroys. In yielding, you find release; in release, you find realignment.

Temple Practice
Write one area where you are struggling to let go. Pray aloud, "Not my will, Lord, but Yours be done," and release it into His hands through the Holy Spirit.

Health Coaching Tip
Progressive muscle relaxation mirrors spiritual surrender. Tighten and release each muscle group, symbolizing letting go of control.

Prayer
Holy Spirit,
Teach me to trust God's divine plan more than my preferences. Align my will with His will through Your guidance and peace.
In Jesus' name, I pray, Amen.

Journal Prompt
What happens in your emotions when you truly release control to the Holy Spirit?

Affirmation
I surrender my will to His will; the Holy Spirit guides my path.

 DAY 29 – LIVE IN PURPOSE

Scripture
For we are God's handiwork, created in Christ Jesus to do good works, which God pre-pared in advance for us to do.
(Ephesians 2:10 NIV)

Reflection
The Holy Spirit not only comforts—He commissions. After seasons of suffering, pur-pose can feel distant, yet God never wastes what He has allowed in your life. Every lesson and every scar becomes a tool in His hands. He works it all together for your good and His glory.

You are God's handiwork, created in Christ Jesus to do good works. You are His mas-terpiece—molded and shaped for meaning that extends beyond your pain. The Spirit breathes courage where fear once ruled, turning survival into service. When you follow His leading, purpose does not pressure you; it flows naturally from alignment.

Temple Practice
Ask the Spirit, "How can I serve someone today?" Follow the first gentle prompting you sense.

Health Coaching Tip
Serving others releases feel-good endorphins and fosters joy. Small acts of kindness nourish body, soul, and spirit.

Prayer
Holy Spirit,
Reveal the purpose You have prepared for me. Use my restored body, soul, and spirit to bless others and glorify You.
In Jesus' name, I pray, Amen.

Journal Prompt
How has God transformed your pain into purpose?

Affirmation
I walk in divine purpose; my life is God's masterpiece in motion.

DAY 30 – REFLECT HIS GLORY

Scripture
And we all, who with unveiled faces contemplate the Lord's glory, are being transformed into His image with ever-increasing glory, which comes from the Lord, who is the Spirit.
(2 Corinthians 3:18 NIV)

Reflection
When Christ died and the veil was torn, God's presence was released from the *Holiest of Holies* in the Temple of Jerusalem to dwell within you. The Holy Spirit now radiates His glory through your rebuilt temple—body, soul, and spirit. You are transformed from the inside out by the Holy Spirit. You do not have to chase transformation—you simply reflect it.

Every act of love, forgiveness, or faith becomes light shining through healed cracks. The more you contemplate His goodness, the more His image appears in you. This is the ultimate realignment: spirit to Spirit, glory to glory, wholeness to worship.

Temple Practice
Stand before a mirror and whisper, "The Spirit of the Lord lives in me." Smile in gratitude for the glory He reflects through you.

Health Coaching Tip
Smiling releases serotonin and lifts mood—a physical echo of inner joy. Let gratitude show on your face.

Prayer
Holy Spirit,
Thank You for dwelling within me. Let Your light shine through my life so others see Your glory.
In Jesus' name, I pray, Amen.

Journal Prompt
Where do you see glimpses of God's glory shining through your restored spiritual health?

Affirmation
The Spirit of the Lord lives in me; His glory radiates through my rebuilt temple—body, soul, and spirit.

 Closing Prayer – Realign Your Spirit

Holy Spirit,

Thank You for drawing me close and teaching me to dwell in Your presence.

You have taken what was weary and crushed, and You have breathed new life into my spirit. You have restored my connection with the Father and renewed my strength through Christ.

Thank You for guiding my steps, whispering truth, and filling me with Your peace. Help me remain sensitive to Your voice and obedient to Your leading. When I am tempted to rely on my own strength, remind me to abide in You. When my passion fades, fan the flame again with Your presence.

May my spirit stay aligned with Yours—rooted in love, grounded in truth, and overflowing with grace toward others. Use my life as a living testimony of Your glory.

Holy Spirit, empower me to walk in Your rhythm and reveal Your glory wherever I go.

In Jesus' name, I pray, Amen.

Continue Your Triune Temple Journey™

Congratulations!

You have completed the *Rebuild Your Temple, God's Way® Faith and Health Devotional: A 30-Day Journey to Holistic Health and Wholeness*—a journey through your Triune Human Temple™ from the *Outer Court* to the *Inner Court* to the *Holiest of Holies*.

But you have just begun the transformation process — a journey of holistic healing that continues day by day.

You have rebuilt the *Outer Court* of your temple by restoring your body, renewed *the Inner Court* of your temple by healing your soul, and entered the *Holiest of Holies* of your temple by realigning your spirit with God the Father and God the Son through God the Holy Spirit.

Your Triune Human Temple™ is being restored to health and wholeness —not through perfection, but through His continual presence and grace.

Remember: Healing is not a destination; it is a divine rhythm of abiding, trusting, and growing in His grace.

Continue your Triune Temple Journey™ of faith and health by:

- Abiding in God's presence through worship, Scripture meditation, prayer, and community.

- Practicing the daily rhythms of the new habits you have begun to form— nourishment, movement, rest; surrender, gratitude, peace; communion, harmony, and purpose.

- Serving God and others with your renewed strength—let your story inspire others, stir up their faith and reignite their hope.

Accept the invitation to let **Rebuild Your Temple, God's Way®** continue to guide and support you.

Visit **www.rebuildyourtemplegodsway.com** to explore transformational Christian health coaching programs and resources designed to help you reclaim and maintain a life of health and wholeness—body, soul, and spirit—God's way.

Restore Your Body. Renew Your Soul. Realign Your Spirit.™